Seven Secrets
to Success

RESTORE YOUR SOUL

As Kevin, still bewildered, lay in bed half an hour later, he opened the drawer in the bedside table and removed a large book with a heavily embossed cover. He opened it and discovered that all the pages, except for the first, were blank. On the first page someone had written a brief message in a perfect copperplate script. "Yesterday is gone."

Kevin repeated it out loud. "Yesterday is gone."

He replaced the book in the drawer. It took him less than a minute to fall asleep.

Originally written as a letter from the author to his suicidal friend, this inspiring book has been passed from friend to friend for over 15 years—offering hope to the weary and motivation for us all to let go of the past and follow our dreams.

It is the story of Kevin, who believes his life is over after the failure of his business and marriage. Without the strength or know-how to get back on his feet, he finds himself on a pier, hopeless and ready to jump to his death. Suddenly, like a beacon in a storm, an elderly man named Todd Melvin appears and persuades him to stop and talk about his troubles. As Todd and Kevin's friendship grows, Kevin learns seven simple secrets that help him see life in a whole new light.

As you learn and grow along with the main character, let this heartwarming tale—and these seven secrets to success—restore your soul and bring you a lifetime of happiness!

ABOUT THE AUTHOR

Richard Webster was born in New Zealand in 1946, where he still resides. He travels widely every year, lecturing and conducting workshops around the world. He has written many books, mainly on psychic subjects, and also writes monthly magazine columns.

Richard is married with three children. His family is very supportive of his occupation, but his oldest son, after observing his father's career, has decided to become an accountant.

TO WRITE TO THE AUTHOR

If you wish to contact the author or would like more information about this book, please write to the author in care of Llewellyn Worldwide, and we will forward your request. Both the author and publisher appreciate hearing from you and learning of your enjoyment of this book and how it has helped you. Llewellyn Worldwide cannot guarantee that every letter written to the author can be answered, but all will be forwarded. Please write to:

Richard Webster
c/o Llewellyn Worldwide
P.O. Box 64383, Dept. K797–8,
St. Paul, MN 55164-0383, U.S.A.
Please enclose a self-addressed, stamped envelope for reply,
or $1.00 to cover costs.
If outside the U.S.A., enclose international postal reply coupon.

RICHARD WEBSTER

Seven Secrets to Success

A STORY OF HOPE

1997
LLEWELLYN PUBLICATIONS
ST. PAUL, MINNESOTA, U.S.A. 55164-0383

FIRST EDITION
First Printing, 1997

Cover design by Lisa Novak
Cover Photo by Index Stock, Jan Halaska
Editing and design by Connie Hill

Library of Congress Cataloging-in-Publication Data
Webster, Richard, 1946–
    Seven secrets to success : a story of hope / Richard
Webster. — 1st ed.
        p.   cm.   —)
        ISBN 1-56718-797–8 (pbk.)
    1. Success.   2. Conduct of life.   I. Title.
BF637.S8W345   1997
158.1—dc21   97-37699
                                                      CIP

Llewellyn Publications
A Division of Llewellyn Worldwide, Ltd.
St. Paul, Minnesota 55164-0383, U.S.A.

Table of Contents

Introduction — ix

Chapter One — 1

Chapter Two — 9

Chapter Three — 23

Chapter Four — 33

Chapter Five — 53

Chapter Six — 65

Chapter Seven — 71

Chapter Eight — 79

Chapter Nine — 95

Chapter Ten — 101

The Seven Secrets to Success — 113

Other Books by Richard Webster

Feng Shui for Beginners: Successful Living by Design (Llewellyn Publications, 1997)

Dowsing for Beginners: The Art of Discovering Water, Treasure, Gold, Oil, Artifacts (Llewellyn Publications, 1996)

Talisman Magic: Yantra Squares for Tantric Divination (Llewellyn Publications, 1995)

Omens, Oghams & Oracles: Divination in the Druidic Tradition (Llewellyn Publications, 1995)

Revealing Hands: How to Read Palms (Llewellyn Publications, 1994)

How to Develop Psychic Power (Martin Breese Ltd., 1988)

How to Read Minds (Brookfield Press, 1984)

Discovering Numerology (Brookfield Press, 1983)

How to Read Tea Leaves (Brookfield Press, 1982)

The Stars and Your Destiny (Brookfield Press, 1982)

Sun Sign Success (Brookfield Press, 1982)

Forthcoming from the Author

Chinese Numerology: The Magic Numbers of Master Wu

Astral Travel for Beginners

Spirit Guides & Angel Guardians

Feng Shui Series

Introduction

I wrote this story some fifteen years ago to help a friend of mine who was going through a difficult time. He had completely withdrawn from his friends and family and was not willing to talk with anyone. However, he had always been a keen reader and I thought it might be possible to get through to him by writing a letter.

When I sat down to write it, the story of Kevin began to unfold. I was surprised—and delighted— at how quickly my friend responded to this story. He came out of his depression and began life anew.

He asked my permission to make copies of *Seven Secrets to Success* to give to other people he knew who were having difficulties in their life, and over the years I have come across many people who have been helped by the story. When people asked me why it wasn't available in a more permanent form, I always replied that it was intended to be simply a letter to a friend.

Recently, another friend needed help, so I dusted off the original manuscript, updated it, removed the personal information that was relevant only to the person I had originally written it for, and gave it to her. Happily, she also responded to the ideas and suggested that I offer it to a wider market.

Here it is. I hope you will find it just as helpful as you progress through life.

————

Chapter
1

The rain started again as Kevin walked out on to the jetty. He pulled his rain coat around him and lowered his head. The wind was relentless, seeming to come from every direction, whipping the harbor into noisy, cream-frothed waves.

Rain trickled down Kevin's back and he pulled his coat more tightly around his neck. He stood in the reflection of the solitary light and looked at the blackness around him. Here he was, alone again, and tonight it seemed as if the world was empty.

To his right he could see the headlights of cars as they headed toward the city, but the only sounds he could hear were the waves breaking on the beach and the wind as it howled round the old derelict wooden building at the end of the jetty. Kevin remembered when it used to be a proud building and the judges of the yacht races would gather there to watch the boats race on the harbor. Like him, the building had seen better times.

A wave of self-pity added tears to the rain on his face and Kevin rubbed his eyes vigorously before moving out of the light and down toward the end of the jetty.

A stray cat hissed at Kevin and ran from its shelter beneath a bench as he approached. Kevin felt sorry for it, but did not stop his slow, steady pace toward the end of the jetty.

It was quieter at the end. The old building protected him from much of the wind and some of the rain. A mile across the harbor he could see the lights of houses on the other shore—all containing people getting on with their lives.

Kevin looked down at the water, black, creamy with foam, creating strange pictures on the frantically tossing surface. It looked cold, but was strangely inviting, too.

Kevin began to take his rain coat off, but it seemed a ludicrous idea and he fastened the top buttons again.

The water seemed hypnotic, the waves striking the old palings of the jetty before being sucked out again. In and out, in and out.

Kevin thought he heard a voice, but he couldn't relate to it. No one knew he was here. He heard the voice again. It was much closer now. He turned and was surprised to see a figure heading toward him. It looked like a frail old man. What could he be doing out on a night like this?

As he came closer Kevin saw the man was very old. And he wasn't dressed for the rain, either. He was wearing casual trousers and an open-necked shirt. His clothes and hair were drenched. Kevin sighed. Just when he wanted to be alone, wasn't it typical that someone else happened to be on the jetty.

The man stopped beside him and looked down at the water. He shivered and then looked earnestly up at Kevin.

"Don't do it," he said. "Don't do it."

The old man took a few steps back and stopped, looking at Kevin. He seemed totally unaware of the howling wind and driving rain.

"Go away," Kevin said.

The man stepped forward again. Kevin noticed how incredibly thin the old man was. His saturated clothes clung to him like a second layer of skin.

"Look," the man said. "I live just over there."
He turned and pointed at a large, well-lit block of
apartments overlooking the harbor. "Come back
with me and have a cup of coffee. If you want
someone to talk to, I'll be happy to listen."

Kevin looked at the apartments and then back to
the sea. Why could he never do anything properly?
He became aware that the old man was shivering.

"All right," he said gruffly. "I could do with
some coffee."

The old man's apartment was on the third floor
and in good weather the windows would have provided a fabulous view of the harbor and city.

Kevin walked around the large living room as
the old man busied himself in the kitchen. Kevin
was used to home comforts, but this man had to be
extremely wealthy to maintain an apartment like
this one, he thought. Comfortable leather-uphol-
stered furniture surrounded an antique coffee
table. On one wall was a bookcase. The other two
walls were crowded with paintings. The man was
obviously an art collector. Kevin knew little about
art, but recognized the names of some of the
artists. The fourth wall consisted of windows and
large sliding glass doors that opened out onto a
balcony overlooking the harbor. The sounds of the

storm barely reached through the large doors. An antique brass telescope stood on a tripod before the door. *So that's how he saw me*, Kevin thought.

The man returned, holding a tray which he carefully put down on the coffee table.

"Sit down," he said to Kevin. "Are you hungry?"

"No, no I'm not. Thanks." Kevin sat down awkwardly and poured two cups of coffee from a silver jug. "Do you take milk?" he asked.

The old man smiled and nodded. He sat down opposite Kevin and took the cup.

"Thanks," he said.

The old man had changed into dry clothes and looked considerably larger now, dressed in a heavy, multi-colored sweater and pale blue trousers. He had dried and brushed his distinguished-looking silver hair and now appeared more like the owner of this luxurious apartment than the sodden, bedraggled old man who had found Kevin on the wharf.

He looked seriously at Kevin. His face was long and thin. His eyes were blue and seemed to belong to a much younger man. They matched a wide mouth that seemed set in a permanent smile. Not a cynical or supercilious smile, Kevin thought. Just the smile of a happy man who is faintly amused at what he sees.

"Welcome to my home," the man said. "My name's Todd Melvin." The old man offered his right hand and Kevin shook it.

"I'm Kevin. Kevin Huddersfield."

Todd sipped his coffee and looked at Kevin over the cup.

"I take it that things are not going too well for you, Kevin."

He had a soft, melodious voice, Kevin thought. A slight accent. What was it? English?

"Not too well," Kevin agreed.

"Want to talk about it?"

Kevin shook his head. "I'm not very good at sharing my problems," he said.

Todd nodded. "That's fine," he said. "I used to be just like you, you know. I'd bottle everything up inside, keep it all to myself. I don't do that now." He took another sip of his coffee. "How old are you, Kevin?"

"Twenty-eight."

"Twenty-eight," Todd repeated. "I'm fifty years older than you! What I'd give to be twenty-eight again."

Kevin looked around the room. "But you've done all right," he said. "You're successful."

Todd smiled. "Yes," he agreed. "I guess I am. But when I was twenty-eight I felt I had nothing, nothing at all."

"Neither have I."

Todd laughed. "That's what I thought when I was your age," he said. "But I was wrong, just as you are. You have youth, you have energy, you have dreams. And you have time. How wonderful to have time!"

"I have youth," Kevin agreed. "And I had dreams."

"And they were shattered?"

Kevin nodded. Despite himself he felt tears coming to his eyes, and then he was sobbing uncontrollably. Todd waited until he stopped and then passed him a clean handkerchief.

"I think maybe you should talk," he said quietly.

This time Kevin agreed. The story came out in a disjointed fashion, but at the end of it Todd knew all about Kevin's business failure, the dishonesty of his business partner, and the breakup of his marriage.

"I understand," Todd said in the silence once Kevin had finished. He held up a hand as Kevin started to speak. "Now I understand why you were on that jetty tonight. Tell me, Kevin, did it help to talk about your problems?"

"I, I think so."

"Good. Now I have no idea if you have any-where to go tonight, but I have a spare room you can use. We can talk further in the morning."

"You're offering me a room for the night?"

Todd smiled. "Of course. It's a horrible night outside, and I wouldn't want to continue this con-versation on the jetty. It's better for both of us if you sleep here tonight. Okay?"

"Thanks, Mr. Melvin."

"My name's Todd. Here, let me show you your room."

As Kevin, still bewildered, lay in bed half an hour later, he opened the drawer in the bedside table and removed a large book with a heavily embossed cover. He opened it and discovered that all the pages, except for the first, were blank. On the first page someone had written a brief message in a flowing, handwritten script. "Yesterday is gone."

Kevin repeated it out loud. "Yesterday is gone."

He replaced the book in the drawer. It took him less than a minute to fall asleep.

———

Yesterday is gone.

Chapter 2

It was nine o'clock when Kevin woke up. He quickly showered, dressed in clothes that Todd had loaned him the night before, and went through to the living room.

The sliding glass doors were open and Todd was standing on the balcony looking out across the harbor. He turned and smiled as Kevin stepped through the door. Todd gestured at the scene.

"Look at the lovely morning after that storm! Isn't it a glorious view?"

Kevin looked down at the passing cars. Apart from some debris on the road there was little evidence of the wind and rain of the night before. The harbor was azure in color and hundreds of small yachts darted across the smooth surface.

"It's Saturday," Kevin said. "These must be the kids out practicing."

"That's right," Todd agreed. "Apart from the extra traffic on the roads, I love the weekends. In fact, every day has its own charm."

The two men stood in silence, gazing across the harbor at the buildings on the far side. Above it the clear blue sky played host to a few small, fluffy clouds.

Kevin sighed. "It's a lovely morning."

Todd glanced at him. "Every morning is a lovely morning," he said. "Particularly when you get to be my age! You know, I can stand or sit here for hours, no matter what the weather is like. It's all beautiful." He indicated a chair. "Sit down and relax. I've got your breakfast ready."

Kevin nodded and sat down. Somehow, this morning he felt awkward in this man's company. He tried to put his thoughts into words as he drank the freshly squeezed orange juice that Todd placed before him, and ate a bowl of muesli.

"You've been so kind to me," he began.

Todd smiled and waved his hands deprecatingly.

"Why? Why have you been so good? You don't know me."

"Surely it's my duty as a human being to help someone who seems to need it," Todd replied quietly.

"I see that. But not many people would do what you did. I could have mugged you out on the jetty. I could have stolen things from your home while you slept."

"But you didn't."

"No." Kevin finished the cereal and placed the tray to one side. His eyes caught the telescope. "Are you looking for people who are desperate enough to commit suicide?" he asked.

Todd looked across the harbor at the flag flying on its mast on the headland on the other side.

"No. Not really," he said slowly. "But I must admit I enjoy helping others."

"Have there been others like me?"

Todd nodded. "A few. I've been living here for ten years now, and occasionally, usually in bad weather, someone will walk out onto that jetty just the way you did. You know, I can tell from here what they intend doing. It's just their body language, I think. Something about the way they carry themselves."

"Was I like that?"

"Oh, yes, very much so." Todd stood up. "Tea or coffee?"

"Tea, thanks."

Kevin watched Todd go through to the kitchen. After a moment he joined him.

"How do you keep everything so clean?" he asked, looking admiringly around the large, spotless kitchen.

"Aha! When you get to my age you have time," Todd said. "Plus, I have a lady come in every couple of days to clean. She'll be here soon. She's the one who deserves the credit."

"Before I went to sleep last night I looked in the drawer beside my bed. There was a book there, with just a few words written in it."

"That's right. Do you remember them?"

"Sure. They are: 'Yesterday is gone.' They are the only words in the whole book!"

"But it's enough. Don't you think that's exactly the right number of words to have in that book?"

"Agreed." Kevin watched Todd pour the tea. "But those three words. They could have been written just for me!"

"They were."

Kevin followed Todd back to the living room. "But Todd, the ink is faded; those words were written in that book years ago!"

"They were written for you, Kevin. My wife wrote those words in that book many years ago. Those three words were what I needed then. The same three words are needed by you now. Live your life today, Kevin! Yesterday is gone, and who knows if either of us will see tomorrow."

"I want to thank you for letting me see today."

Todd shook his head. "It was meant to be," he said. "I can't take any credit for that."

Kevin shook his head in bewilderment. "I can't understand half of what you say!" he said. "I was planning to kill myself last night. You stopped me!"

"Yes." Todd was silent for a long while. "But look at it this way. What made you think of drowning yourself? There are better ways of committing suicide."

"I didn't know what I was doing. I was just wandering around."

"Looking for me."

"But I didn't know you were here!"

"Let's just call it karma."

"Karma? Isn't that some strange Eastern religion?"

Todd laughed. "No. It's simply cause and effect. Whatever energy you put out, you get back. Put out good and sometime, somewhere, it will come back to you. Put out bad, and the same thing will happen. What's the matter, Kevin? You've gone pale."

Kevin gulped some tea. "I don't know where you've come from, Todd, but I've never met anyone like you before. You make me see things in different ways. When I woke up this morning I thought, well, I'm still alive. Now I can get even with my partner."

"Get even?"

"Yeah. Give him the comeuppance he deserves. He robbed me blind. It's his fault the business failed. He...."

"Calm down, Kevin."

Kevin noticed his shoulders were suddenly tense. He stood up and stretched.

"But now you seem to have read my mind, and you're telling me that if I get even, I will pay for it later. Isn't that what you're saying?"

"I guess so. Look, Kevin, I know nothing about your business and what your partner did or didn't do. But you told me that the business is gone. It no longer trades. It's history. It belongs to yesterday, and...."

"Yesterday is gone."

Todd laughed. "You're getting it, aren't you? Okay, it belongs to yesterday. Now think about this. Let's say you get even with your partner. I don't know how you'd do that, but let's suppose you had him arrested and placed in jail. Would you consider that getting even?"

Kevin nodded slowly. "I guess so."

"What would that do to you?"

"Well, I don't know. I guess I could then forget about him and start building my life again."

"Okay. Now, how long will it take you to get the evidence to put him behind bars?"

"I have no idea. I don't even know if I could find the evidence now."

"So it might take three months, or even a year."

"That's right. And maybe I wouldn't find the information I need."

"So you might spend years searching."

"I'd kill him first!"

Todd smiled. "That would do a lot of good. You'd be the one behind bars then! Now, look at it this way. Maybe your partner is guilty of these terrible things and maybe he isn't. No, please hear me out," he added as Kevin started to interject. "Either way, your life is on hold while you get more and more bitter and twisted trying to find proof. Is that living? Even if you find the evidence and he goes to prison, what have you done to your life?"

"I'd have put the lying crook behind bars!"

"How much satisfaction would that give you?"

"Plenty!"

Todd laughed. "Think about it a while. And while you are doing that, think about this. Suppose you spend the next twelve months trying to get even with your partner. That's fine. One year of your life has gone. Now, think about letting go of the past."

"Yesterday is gone."

"Quite right. Let go of the past and start again. One year from now you'll be well on track to whatever your goals might be. So, which is better? Getting on with your life, or getting even?"

Kevin squirmed uncomfortably in his chair. "You make life so difficult!"

Todd laughed again. "I think I do the opposite. Look, your friend has taken advantage of you. Actually, he did more than that—he almost ended your life. Last night was a horrible, dirty, wet evening—like your life was then. But look at this morning!" Todd waved toward the glistening harbor. "Today the world is new again. It's a new world, full of opportunity and promise. It's precious. It's a gift to you and anyone else who decides to take advantage of it. Yesterday is gone. Leave yesterday where it belongs. You need to live in the here and now. You need to make plans for the future, but the only time you really have is now."

"Thank you." Kevin found it hard to meet Todd's steady gaze. He studied the pattern on the slippers Todd had given him to wear. After a while, he said, "What has all this got to do with karma?"

"I'm glad you asked," Todd said. "How about going for a walk and we'll discuss it."

"Karma is an abstruse concept that has been around forever, in every religion and philosophy," Todd continued as they walked slowly around the waterfront, on the sidewalk between the beach and the road. Kevin noticed that everyone seemed to know his new friend. Their faces would light up when they saw him, and people would come across simply to say hello.

"Now I'm not a religious man in the usual sense of the word, Kevin. I believe in reincarnation and I believe in karma. I don't expect you to necessarily go along with reincarnation, but it is vital that you understand karma.

"Karma is the law of giving and receiving. What you put out, you get back. Not always in a clearly recognizable way, of course. For instance, many, many years ago someone helped me during a difficult time. I vowed then that, given the opportunity, I would do the same to others."

"And you are doing that with me."

"In a small way, perhaps, I am. But I believe it was meant to be. You see, if you'd gone out on that jetty earlier, I would not have seen you as I had dinner at a friend's house. If you'd been much later, I wouldn't have seen you either, as I'd have been in bed."

"So I was lucky?"

Todd chuckled. "Now that's a whole new concept! We make our own luck, Kevin, with what we feel and expect and think about. Actually, I was the lucky one, as I was there at the right time to be able to help."

Kevin shook his head. "I don't see it that way. I'll always be very, very grateful to you, Todd."

"Thanks, but it's not necessary. I've been repaid already with the changes I've seen in you so far." Todd stopped to talk with a mother and daughter for a few moments. Kevin noticed the genuine affection of both as they hugged the old man. *One day I'll be like him*, Kevin thought.

The two men resumed walking in silence. After a while, Todd said, "See that old oak tree over there?"

"Yes. It's beautiful."

"Did you know that several years ago developers wanted to pull it down to build apartments on the site?"

"Thank goodness they didn't succeed."

"That's right. But it took a lot of effort by many, many people to stop it happening. They did something really worthwhile. It's probably very small in the whole scheme of things, but it makes the world a better place. It fills me with delight just to look at that tree."

Todd stopped walking. "Let's cross the road and see it close up."

Kevin smiled. "Sure, why not?"

While they waited for a pause in the traffic, Todd told Kevin how the ancient druids used to worship trees, particularly oak trees. "They believed that the roots went down to the underworld, while the trunk lived in this world, and the branches reached up toward the heavens. Consequently, trees lived in all three worlds at the same time. Come on, let's go."

With surprising agility, Todd crossed the road, followed by Kevin.

It was pleasantly cool in the shade under the old tree. Todd looked up into its branches with awe.

"Isn't it gorgeous?" he whispered.

Kevin had never looked at a tree this way before. Yet he somehow sensed what Todd was saying.

"Yes, it sure is."

"Touch it."

Kevin reached out and touched the trunk.

"Good. Now give it a big hug."

"What!"

"A really big hug. Like this." Todd extended his arms and hugged the trunk for several seconds. When he let go his eyes were glowing. "Now it's your turn."

Kevin reluctantly and tentatively hugged the tree.

"Not like that. You wouldn't hug a close friend like that. Pretend it's a good friend. That's better."

Kevin hugged the tree for a while and, as he did, felt a strange feeling inside himself.

"Well?" Todd asked when Kevin had stopped looking around to see if anyone had seen what he was doing. "What did it feel like?"

Kevin looked embarrassed. "It wasn't what I expected at all. The tree seemed to give me a bit of a lift."

"It restored your soul."

"Yes, you could say that."

"Do you know why?"

Kevin shook his head.

"Because the tree is alive. It responds to what you say, even what you think. And, of course, it responds to your hugs."

"Is this something you learned from the druids?" Kevin was deliberately flippant, but Todd answered it seriously.

"In a way, yes. I read about it in a book somewhere. To begin with, I was like you, reluctant to try it. Then I became a night-time hugger, hugging trees in the dark when no one could see me. Now, I don't care. I just hug trees wherever I go. It's one of the advantages of being old. People ignore your idiosyncrasies! Remember though, Kevin, that you can be restored and revitalized any time you want by hugging a tree. I guess it's better to hug a good friend, but when friends are hard to find, hug a tree."

Silently, they walked back to Todd's apartment, Kevin deep in thought. At the entrance, he spoke.

"Todd, you've changed my life. I've never met anyone like you before. Thank you, thank you so much."

"That's fine, Kevin. Come up and have some lunch, and then you'll have to excuse me. I've things I have to do."

"Shall I go now?"

"No. It would be good to have company for lunch. You do have somewhere to go, don't you?"

"Of course. I'll go home."

Later, when Kevin left, Todd made him promise to visit the following day.

"Remember the things we discussed," he said. "Today is all we have. Live in the present, not the past. Let the past be. Also, hug life. Not just trees, though that's important, too. Hug life, all of it. And never let an opportunity for a hug go by without taking it. Okay?"

Kevin's eyes were moist. He gave Todd a bear hug.

"See, I am learning," Kevin said as he released Todd.

———

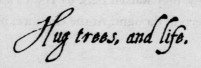

Chapter 3

Promptly, at seven, Kevin pressed the doorbell for Todd's apartment. Just as he was about to press it again, Todd answered it. His voice was crackly over the intercom.

"Is that who I think it is?"

"Yes, Todd. It's me, Kevin."

"Come on up." Kevin heard the door unlock and let himself in. He ran up the stairs, in preference to the elevator. Above Todd's front door he saw a Chinese yin-yang symbol, surrounded by figures made from three parallel lines. He was still looking at it when Todd opened the door.

"Ah, welcome, Kevin. I see you're looking at my pakua."

"Pakua? I bet I'm going to learn more tonight." Impulsively, Kevin hugged Todd. Afterwards, Todd studied Kevin carefully.

"You're looking a lot better," he said.

Kevin laughed. "In just twenty-four hours?"

Todd nodded. "That's the first time I've heard you laugh. It's a great sound. You should laugh a lot more. We all should, you know. It's great for mental and physical health. And, I wouldn't be surprised, for spiritual health, too."

Todd escorted Kevin into the living room and poured two whiskeys. He explained that his cleaning lady was cooking the dinner tonight, to give them an opportunity to talk.

"Come outside onto the balcony."

It was a mild evening and the setting sun cast a soft golden glow over the scene. Kevin's eyes were immediately drawn to the jetty. Several people were fishing from it, taking advantage of the high tide. Sounds of children's voices and happy laughter came up to them on the breeze.

"This is heaven," Kevin said.

"It is, indeed," Todd agreed. "I made up my mind to live here many years ago. It took a long time, but here I am, and it's as close to heaven as I want to get right now!"

Kevin leaned over and watched the traffic moving slowly below them.

"It's always busy," Todd said. "But especially during the weekends. People out for a drive, or looking for somewhere to eat, or walk. It's a popular route."

"Don't you wish it were quieter sometimes?"

Todd shook his head. "No. The nice thing is that most people who drive past here are intent on having fun. Sure, we get the commuters every morning and night, but the rest of the time, people drive along here for pleasure, and I like that. I think that maybe I pick up their happy vibes."

Kevin smiled. "It wouldn't surprise me in the least."

Todd chuckled and Kevin joined in.

"Dinner's served."

Kevin turned to meet Todd's cleaning lady, a strikingly attractive lady in her middle forties. She held out her hand to him.

"Hi! My name's Elspeth. You must be Kevin."

"Yes. How do you do."

"Ah, a real gentleman!" Elspeth gave a mock curtsey. "Come on in."

The table was set for three, Kevin noticed, and once the meals were served Elspeth sat down and ate with them. She was obviously very fond of Todd, paying him constant attention and frequently touching him. Kevin felt a tiny touch of envy as he watched. *That's crazy,* he told himself. *Why should I be envious of an old man and a middle-aged lady?*

Elspeth was good company. She told Kevin about being widowed and bringing up two children on her own in such an amusing way that Kevin found himself laughing frequently.

"Now it's your turn," Elspeth told him, reaching over and touching him gently on the back of his hand. "Tell me about you."

"There's not much to tell," Kevin said. "I was born not far from here, twenty-eight years ago. I was married, but we are separated now. And I was in business, the computer business, until a month or so ago."

Elspeth patted his hand gently. "And what are you going to do now?"

Kevin shook his head. "You know, I really don't know. It's all been so sudden." Abruptly, he felt tears prick his eyes and he looked down at his plate so the others could not see.

"Poor dear," he heard Elspeth say.

After coffee, served in the living room, Elspeth washed the dishes and left. She kissed both Todd and Kevin on the cheek.

"Good luck!" she said to Kevin.

"She's your, er, cleaning lady?" Kevin said, once she had gone.

Todd chuckled. "She's my housekeeper, my cleaning lady, and my conscience."

"Nothing more?"

"Isn't that enough? Oh well, I didn't think it was that obvious. She's everything to me."

"But she doesn't live here."

"That's her choice, not mine." Todd cleared his throat and changed the subject. "What did you do yesterday afternoon and today?"

"I went home and went over a few things. I did the laundry, fed the cat, went to bed early."

"And today?"

"Fed the cat. Stayed in bed most of the morning. Oh, I hugged a tree this afternoon!"

Todd smiled. "That's good! Did you feel better afterwards?"

"Yes, I think so. It made me think about the other things you told me. Leaving the past behind. It's hard to do."

"I know. Keep working on it. You'll get there."

"I hope so. Then I went back home, spruced myself up a bit and came here."

"And what about tomorrow?"

"What about tomorrow?"

"What are you doing tomorrow?"

Kevin shook his head and grimaced. "I've no idea."

"Do you know what that means?"

"What?"

"It means that tomorrow will be a wasted day, just like most of today. What do you have that I don't have? Time, that's what you have. At your age, with your health, you have time on your side. You have to use it wisely. It's a crime to waste too much time. I want you to waste some time, Kevin. Don't get me wrong. We all need time to relax and unwind and do nothing. But that's not what you were doing today. You were hiding from reality, and you were wasting precious time."

"What should I have done?"

Todd spread his hands out wide. "All sorts of things. You could have phoned your wife and told her how your cat was. Then you could have discussed other things. You could have phoned your

accountant and found out what's happening with
your business windup. You could have done some
constructive thinking about the future. Tell me,
how long is your money going to last?"

"Not long."

"A week, a month, a year?"

"A month, maybe a little longer."

"That's good. You have some breathing space
there. Now, let's assume you have six weeks. What
do you want to achieve in the next six weeks?"

"I've no idea."

Todd shook his head. "That's crazy. Didn't you
set goals while you were in business? If you didn't,
you deserved to fail. I want you to go into my
study and sit down at my desk. You'll find paper
and envelopes there. Write down all the things you
intend doing in the next six weeks. Then seal them
in an envelope and give the envelope to me. I
promise I won't look in the envelope, and I'll give
it back to you in six weeks' time."

"You're a tyrant, you know that," Kevin said,
but he dutifully went to Todd's study. Before sitting down he looked at several of the books on the
bookshelves that lined every wall.

There were books on self-improvement and psychology, books on salesmanship and management, books on English literature and poetry, and a large collection of books on current affairs and politics. On the bottom shelf of one wall was a large selection of thrillers and adventure stories. Kevin smiled. At least Todd owned some books that he had also read.

Thirty minutes later he returned and handed a sealed envelope to Todd. Todd accepted it gravely and placed it under a ceramic rabbit on his mantelpiece.

"Was it hard?" he asked.

"It was all right once I got going," Kevin said. "The hardest part was thinking forward into the future."

"Good. Actually, you were setting some goals for yourself."

Kevin nodded. "I used to be good at that."

"Uh huh. Did you set goals for your marriage?"

"No. Just business goals."

Todd smiled. "You're a typical businessman! Tell me, did you put some personal goals into that envelope?"

"Yes, I did."

"That's excellent, Kevin. I'm proud of you. Did you know that virtually no one sets goals for themselves? If you don't know where you want to be, how will you know the route to get there? It's the saddest thing. It's such a colossal waste. We all have so much potential in our brains. Yet, virtually no one does a simple exercise like making plans for the future. I believe around five per cent of people set goals for themselves. That means ninety-five per cent of the world's population set no goals." Todd patted Kevin on the shoulder. "Well, you've now learned number three."

"I see. Live for today. Hug trees and life. And set goals. Tell me, Todd, how many rules are there?"

"Seven, so you're almost halfway there. And they're not rules. I regard them as stepping stones. You don't have to keep to them, but if you don't you get wet!" Todd looked at his watch. "It's not late, but you have an envelope full of goals to start working on, so you'd better go. How about we meet again the same time next week." He laughed at the expression on the younger man's face. "I know, it would be good to see you tomorrow and the next day. But can't you see, some things you have to do on your own. During this week set some longer term goals for yourself. And if you want to, you can tell me about them next week. I'm really looking forward to hearing what you do this week!"

———————————

Set worthwhile goals.

Chapter
4

For three days Kevin stayed motivated. He visited his accountant and made arrangements to pay back debts. He phoned his wife twice and on the second call told her how much he loved her.

"Would you like to come for dinner?" Sandy asked.

Kevin was so surprised that it was hard to speak. "Dinner? At your parents?"

"Of course. Can you come tonight? About six thirty."

"I, I, I guess so. See you then."

Sandy opened the door when he arrived. She was wearing the blue summer dress that he loved. She looked so beautiful that he stood and gaped.

"Aren't you coming in?"

"Yes. Sorry." He bent to kiss her as he came in, but she moved to one side and extended a hand. He shook it briefly and then kissed it.

"Hello, Kevin. How are you?"

Monica, Sandy's mother, looked him up and down with distaste. Her lips were pursed, showing her permanent disapproval of most things in the world, and especially Kevin.

"Feeling better and better, thank you," Kevin replied.

"Come on in," Monica said. "Duncan's waiting to see you."

Sandy's father managed a smile when Kevin entered the living room. He waved at the liquor cabinet.

"Help yourself, son," he said.

Kevin noticed that both Sandy and Monica had gone on to the kitchen. He poured himself a modest whiskey and sat down in an armchair next to his father-in-law.

"Got yourself a job yet?" Duncan asked. He patted his ample stomach reflectively.

"Not yet. I'm looking, though."

"Sandy tells me you've met some strange guru."

For a moment Kevin couldn't think who he meant. "You mean Todd?" Kevin laughed. "He's not a guru! He's just a kind old man who's been helping me."

"Putting strange ideas in your head, more like."

Kevin shook his head and sighed. "Quite the opposite. He's helping me get back onto an even keel again. That's all."

"Sandy tells me he has these laws of success."

"They're guidelines. He's told me three so far, but I think there are seven altogether."

"I haven't got where I've got by following any laws or guidelines," Duncan said. "What you need is a good, steady job that'll pay the bills. Then you and Sandy'll have a good life, just like me and Monica."

"I don't want a good, steady job. I want more than that."

"We're not letting Sandy go back to a dreamer. You need to face facts, Kevin. Life's hard. It's tough. You need a good, safe, secure job with a regular paycheck every week."

"Just like you?"

Duncan patted his stomach again. "Just like me." He smiled at Kevin. "I haven't done so bad."

Yes, Kevin thought. *Thirty years working for a milk processing plant had provided Duncan with a modest house, a nagging wife, and a spoiled daughter. There might be some money in the bank, but he lived with the constant threat of losing his job to technology.*

"I want more," Kevin said.

Duncan looked at him with surprise. "More?" His voice rose. "More? What more there could there be?"

Kevin shook his head. "I don't know," he muttered. "I wish I did."

Dinner was a lengthy ordeal. Duncan repeatedly told Kevin to give up his dreams and get a job, any job. Monica looked disapproving and kept shaking her head. Sandy kept her head lowered and ate in silence.

"What about your partner," Duncan said as Monica cleared the dessert plates from the table. "Have you got enough evidence yet?"

"I've decided to let that go. It's better to close that door and move ahead."

"Is this more from your guru?"

"He's not my bloody guru!" Kevin realized he was shouting. "I'm sorry. I didn't mean to shout. Todd is helping me, which is more than any of you are."

Duncan and Monica exchanged glances. "I think you'd better leave, young man," Monica said. "If you don't appreciate what we're trying to do for you, it's best that you go."

Kevin went over the evening endlessly as he lay sleepless in bed. Maybe he was being unapprecia- tive. He should have looked at things from their point of view. They saw a young man married to their daughter who had failed in business. It was natural that they wanted security for Sandy. But it was his life. If he wanted more from life than Dun- can did, surely he had the right to try and get it. On the other hand, was he being overly influenced by Todd? Could seven rules, or stepping stones as Todd called them, really work?

Feeling more confused than ever, Kevin finally fell asleep as daybreak came. His cat woke him at lunchtime, licking his face to tell him it was time to get up.

Kevin busied himself around the house to try to avoid thinking, but by the evening he felt depressed again. He picked up the phone and dialed Todd's number, then hung up before anyone answered. He gazed around his living room, almost bare now that Sandy had taken away all of her belongings.

The lack of ornaments and furniture made him think about the failure of his business and marriage, and his lack of future prospects.

"I'll go hug a tree," he told himself.

It was a cool evening, with a few traces of mist hanging in the air. Kevin walked briskly to keep warm, and as he walked his spirits rose.

For the first time in weeks he began to think seriously about his future. The problem was, he didn't know what he wanted to do. And he was still living partly in yesterday.

The park looked forlorn in the half light. Even the trees seemed to droop. The scene looked sad and faintly sinister.

Kevin left the path and walked over the softly yielding grass to the grove of trees.

For a moment, he felt scared, a child frightened of the bogey man. He grinned at the memory of seeing himself as a five- or six-year-old, carefully checking under his bed to see if anyone or anything was hiding there.

He reached out and touched the first tree. It didn't feel right. Kevin moved deeper into the darkness. The second tree felt better, but still wasn't producing any positive energy. Kevin wondered if there were any oak trees in the park. The third tree felt better, but it was thin and spindly. However, it appeared to respond to Kevin's touch.

On an impulse he put both arms around it and hugged it tightly. The tree did respond! It appeared to grow straighter and Kevin could feel the energy surging through the trunk. Or was he just imagining it?

He let go for a moment and then hugged the tree again. Yes, it was real. The tree was responding to his touch, and Kevin felt his depression slowly easing. He hugged the tree for a long time.

"Thank you," he said softly as he let go.

He stepped back to try and see the tree more clearly, as he wanted to recognize it again. As he did, he tripped over something and landed flat on his back.

Kevin was so stunned that he forgot to swear. And then whatever it was he had tripped over started to move.

"My God!" Kevin breathed. He clambered to his feet, heart beating like an express train. Then he paused and looked closer. It was a body! Gently, he prodded it with his foot and the body let out a small cough.

His panic forgotten, Kevin knelt by the still figure and almost gagged. Whoever it was hadn't washed for a long, long time.

"Are you all right?"

The figure did not answer.

Kevin shook it gently by the shoulder.

"Aaahhh!" The sound came out somewhere between a gasp and a prolonged sigh.

"Are you all right?"

The figure began to move and slowly sat up. With eyes now accustomed to the dark, Kevin stared at an elderly man with shoulder-length gray hair. He was wearing a long, dark, foul-smelling overcoat.

The man coughed for a full minute, his body shaking with the effort.

"Do you need help?" Kevin asked once the coughing ceased. The man was obviously a derelict, some bum who lived in the park. An alcoholic, probably.

"What do you think?" the man said bitterly. He grinned at Kevin, revealing a mouth full of rotten teeth and almost gagging Kevin with the stench of his breath.

Kevin stood up to leave.

"You wake me up, ask if you can help, and then just go?" the man said. "What are you doing here anyway?"

"I wish I knew," Kevin said. "Look, I live thirty minutes' walk away. Do you want a bath and a place to sleep tonight?"

"A bloody do-gooder," the man said with disgust. "Go away."

"I can get you some food."

"Go away and let me sleep."

The man settled down inside his large overcoat and prepared to go back to sleep. Kevin looked at him for a while and then slowly walked home.

His spirits soared when he recognized Sandy's car outside the house. She opened the front door as he came up the drive.

"Where've you been?" she asked.

"For a walk," Kevin replied. It did not seem a good time to tell her he'd gone out to hug a tree. "What are you doing here?"

"It's still my home," Sandy said.

"Of course." Kevin desperately wanted to hug her, but she moved aside as he walked in. "Would you like some coffee? We can talk."

Sandy seemed to consider this for a moment. She suddenly smiled and for a moment Kevin caught a glimpse of the wife he loved. He held out his hand. Sandy took it and allowed herself to be led into the living room.

"You weren't your normal self last night," she said after he had made the coffee. "I thought I'd come over and see how you were."

"Thanks," Kevin grinned. "I've been a bit depressed, I guess, but the walk did me good. Seeing you here gives me a lift, too. Also, I've been thinking about Todd's advice. He's helped me so much. I've been trying to work out the other stepping stones to success."

"Oh, Kevin!" Sandy said. "Look, you can't think of success at the moment. You haven't even got a job! Who's going to pay the mortgage on this place next month?"

"But, Sandy, Todd's helping me work on all this. He's made me set some goals, and one of them is finding a job."

"Listen, Kevin." Sandy spoke urgently. "You mustn't get involved in any get-rich-quick sort of thing. Todd's ideas are too airy-fairy. You need to face reality. Get a job, make some money, and then—maybe we can talk about getting back together again."

"So it depends on me making money."

Sandy shook her head and waved her arms wildly. "You're deliberately misunderstanding," she said. "Money has nothing to do with it. You're a dreamer, Kevin, and you can't go through life like that. Sooner or later you have to face up to reality." She drained the last of her coffee and stood up. "Mum and Dad are right. I can't talk to you at the moment. Maybe you just need to hit rock bottom. That's what Dad says. He says it'll either make or break you."

Kevin tossed and turned again in bed that night. Maybe Sandy was right and he was being sucked in to Todd's way of thinking because he was depressed and vulnerable. Perhaps he was just a hopeless dreamer, after all. Sandy seemed to think so. All the same, Sandy obviously had his well-being at heart. Thank goodness he had not told her about hugging trees.

He returned to the park early the following morning. The man was still asleep in the same position. Quietly, Kevin placed a bag of sandwiches and fruit beside the still body, gently touched the tree he had hugged the night before, and left.

He repeated this for the following two mornings, but on the third morning the man was not there.

Kevin explored the entire park, hoping to find him. He passed several other homeless people, but none resembled the first man.

After two hours of searching, Kevin silently placed the package of food next to a middle-aged woman who was sitting on a park bench, bobbing her head up and down in time to some invisible music. She did not even glance in his direction, but he noticed that she bolted the food down as soon as she thought he was out of sight.

Several hours later, Kevin arrived at Todd's apartment. Todd seemed pale and tired, but he listened to Kevin's account of his week with great interest.

"Why did you keep taking that man food?" he asked when Kevin finished.

Kevin shrugged. "Because he needed it, I guess."

"Yet you're short of money."

"Temporarily, I hope," Kevin said. "I guess I took him food because it made me feel good. I felt that there was someone worse off than me, and it felt good to help him."

"So you did it because it made you feel good." The old man nodded his head slowly. "Well, that's as good a reason as any." He grinned at Kevin who was sprawling, relaxed on the leather couch. "You did well."

"Thanks."

Todd laughed. "That's even better. Do you know that a simple 'thanks' means your self-esteem is good?"

Kevin looked surprised. "It's that easy to tell?"

Todd nodded. Kevin noticed that the old man seemed to have shrunk over the last week. His face looked thinner and his suit hung loosely on the old body, but his eyes remained intense and alive.

"Do you remember what you wrote in your envelope last week?"

Kevin raised his eyes and looked at the mantelpiece. The envelope was still there.

"Yes, of course I do."

"They were goals."

"Right."

"How much have you done to achieve them?"

Kevin shook his head and studied the carpet. "It hasn't been easy," he muttered. "I haven't had much time to think about it. Also, who's going to employ me? I'm a failure!"

"Yes, you are, but only if you think you are. I don't see a failure sitting there. I see a young man, full of promise, with the potential for a glittering future."

"Yeah. Right. My in-laws certainly see me as a failure."

"No opportunities came up during this last week?"

Kevin shook his head.

"Okay. I think it's time we went for a walk."

"A walk? We haven't eaten dinner yet."

"Dinner can wait. Now, I might need to lean on you a little. My legs are getting weak."

"Are you sure you should be doing this?" Kevin asked after they had walked half a mile.

"'Should' and 'maybe' and 'try' aren't words in my vocabulary."

"Okay," Kevin sighed.

They stopped and sat on a bench and watched the cars go by. Across the road the restaurants were starting to get busy, and the happy laughter of people eating at tables on the street wafted across to them. Todd pointed at a second-hand bookstore that was closing for the night.

"See that store? It's owned by a friend of mine. Mike's his name. Twenty years ago he was like you. Now he has a good, steady business and he's really happy. You see, he loves books, so what could be better for him than a bookstore? He saw an opportunity and seized it."

"Has he made any money?" Kevin asked.

Todd laughed. "What's money, for goodness sake? He's doing what he loves to do. Isn't that reward enough?"

Kevin shook his head. "I don't think so."

Todd grabbed his arm with sudden strength. "That's good! We now know that you want to make money."

Kevin felt confused. "Hang on. Doesn't every-one?"

Todd laughed again. "We all need money to live in this world of ours, so we all make money. But when you say you want to make money I assume that you mean lots of money."

"It's easy for you to say, Todd. You've obviously got enough."

Todd shook his head. "No one ever gets enough, Kevin. We all want just a little bit more. I have enough for my needs, but you see, that was one of my goals. I don't think it's one of Mike's. He has other goals." Todd let go of Kevin's arm and watched the traffic for a minute. "Let's go and see Mike before he goes home."

Reluctantly, Kevin let Todd escort him across the road to Mike's shop. The front door was still open and a tall, thin man with a waxed moustache was standing in front of the counter. He beamed when he saw Todd, and ran over and enveloped him in a bear hug.

"How good to see you!" he exclaimed. He looked over Todd's shoulder at Kevin and winked. "Good to see you, too," he said.

Mike sat on his counter and smiled at his visitors. "I'm one of Todd's protégés," he told Kevin. "Maybe Todd's told you."

"He said that you own this bookstore because you love books."

"That's a bit of Todd's advice. You must love what you do. It's funny but I'd never thought of that 'til Todd told me."

"I'm learning a lot, too," Kevin said.

"Are you making money?" Todd asked.

Mike grinned. "Enough, I guess. I'll never make a fortune here, but..." He paused as he looked around his well-stocked shelves. "I'm having a great time." He looked at Kevin. "Isn't that what it's all about?"

Kevin nodded slowly. "I still want to make money."

Mike spread his hands. "Good! Do something that you love and make money from it."

"But you're doing something that you love, and you're only getting by!"

Mike laughed. "Yes and no. Most of my money goes back into the business, so eventually I'll make money when I sell. I also collect first editions, and they're appreciating in value."

"So you are making money!"

"The money's nothing, Kevin," Mike explained. "I'd work here for nothing as I love it so much."

When they left Mike's shop Todd smiled at the mystification on Kevin's face.

"You want to make money, Kevin. We've certainly established that. That's a good, positive goal. What else do you want to do?"

"I don't want to work in computers again."

"Okay. I guess we could call that a negative goal. So you know what you don't want, but you don't know what you do want."

"That's about it. I guess I could go back to journalism. That's how I started my career. I don't really want to do that again, either."

"Okay. Now look around you, Kevin. Right at this very moment you are surrounded by opportunities."

Kevin looked around. The street lights had come on, and most of the cars were now simply colorful blurs. From one of restaurants came the sound of country western music.

"Where?"

Todd laughed gently. "Everywhere, Kevin. Let me help you. See this steady stream of cars going past?"

"Sure."

"Okay. How could you benefit from them? You could get a job selling cars. You could valet them. You could arrange parking for them. You could repaint them, repolish them, provide swinging dice to go inside them."

Kevin laughed. "I see. But I don't see myself working with cars."

Todd shrugged. "That's fine. Look at all these stores. You could own one if you wanted. You could work in one. What do the stores need? They need someone to do their window displays. You could paint their signs for them. If you're good at bookwork, you could keep their accounts for them. You could clean their windows, build their shelving, sweep the street outside them. You could provide them with items to sell."

Todd sat down on a chair outside a café and motioned Kevin to join him. He waited for Kevin to respond to his comments.

Kevin grinned at Todd. "I think I've got it! You brought me here to see that there are opportunities everywhere I look. Is that right?"

"Lesson number four," Todd said.

"I wish you hadn't said that"

"Why not?"

"Because it means I'm more than halfway through your list."

"You're more than halfway through the list, but you've hardly begun."

Kevin's smile faded.

"Don't feel sad," Todd continued. "It's taken me seventy-eight years to learn seven lessons. You've learned four in just over a week. Help me get up again. I think it's time we went home."

———

Opportunities are everywhere.

Chapter 5

Kevin had a busy week applying for different positions by mail and on the phone. He was surprised to find that his enthusiasm remained constant, and credited this to the fact that he went for long walks every day and hugged trees. It was getting easier to hug trees all the time, and Kevin no longer looked around to see if anyone was watching before hugging a likely looking tree.

He spent a lot of time on the phone to Sandy and it did not worry him that Monica and Duncan were cold and abrupt when they answered his calls. His positiveness seemed to gradually affect Sandy and their conversations grew longer. He was sure she looked forward to them as much as he did.

He called Todd twice, but each time Elspeth answered the phone and said that Todd was asleep. He accepted this explanation at the time, but one night woke up at three in the morning after a nightmare in which he found that Todd was desperately ill.

Kevin visited Todd again later that morning. Elspeth let him in and escorted him through to Todd's bedroom. It was a large room full of books, but all Kevin saw was Todd lying in the large double bed. He looked small and frail, almost lost in the blankets and covers.

Todd smiled and extended a hand as Kevin came in.

"How nice to see you," he said. His voice was weak, but his eyes sparkled with delight at having a visitor.

Elspeth plumped up the pillows and helped Todd sit up. Kevin took hold of Todd's hand and continued to hold it as he sat down in the chair beside the bed.

"How long have you been bedridden?" Kevin asked, a slight quaver in his voice.

Todd laughed. "I'm not bedridden, Kevin. I'm just feeling a bit tired. I'll be up again tomorrow."

"Good." Kevin nodded his head several times in relief. "Is there anything I can bring you? Or perhaps do for you?"

Todd shook his head. "I need just one thing. I want to know how you're getting on."

Kevin laughed. "Your lessons are bearing fruit. I feel happier than I've been in a long, long while. I'm having lunch with Sandy tomorrow, so that's a step in the right direction. I've applied for three jobs, and just before I left someone phoned and asked me to come in for an interview. Plus, I've met my creditors and have come to arrangements with them all." Kevin squeezed Todd's hand. "I have to thank you for all of that."

Todd smiled. "It sounds as if you're heading in the right direction. Tell me about the jobs you've applied for."

"Well, the one I'm being interviewed for is a sales position. I'd be selling office equipment."

"Is that what you want to do?"

"Probably not, but beggars can't be choosers."

"Don't ever think like that, Kevin! Your mind attracts to you whatever you think about. You know that." Todd seemed to exhaust what energy he had in saying this, and slumped back onto the pillows, breathing heavily.

"Are you all right?"

"Yes," Todd gasped. "Did you hear what I said?"

Kevin smiled. "You're a tough nut, you are! Yes, I heard you, and you're right. You always are."

Todd shook his head. "That's not true, Kevin. I've made as many mistakes as anyone, probably more than most. You have to question everything I say. I'm not the local oracle or wise man. I'm just me."

"Thank God for that."

"We'll talk about that in a moment. First, tell me about the other jobs."

Kevin haltingly told Todd about the sales position selling roofing materials, and the warehouse manager's position in a stationery supply house. When he finished Todd slowly shook his head.

"These are just short-term positions," Kevin finished. "Just to help me get back on my feet."

"Is that fair to the people who employ you?"

"People change jobs all the time."

"Uh huh." Todd was silent for a long time. "You need to clarify your goals a bit more, I think. Ask Elspeth to fetch you some paper."

Todd waited until Kevin was sitting down again before speaking.

"On the first sheet write down one thing about yourself. Who are you?"

Kevin made a face. "I don't really know who I am."

Todd chuckled. "Of course you do. Even someone who has never met you would know a couple of things about you."

"Really?"

"Of course! You're a human being, aren't you? And you're a man. Write them down." Todd watched as Kevin wrote them down. "Okay," he continued. "What else?"

He watched as Kevin wrote down his own name.

"Good. Already we're up to three. What else?"

Kevin sighed and fiddled with the pen. "I don't know," he said after a while.

"Okay," said Todd. "Put down your nationality. Good. Put down your age. The other night you told me you wanted to be wealthy. Write down 'wealthy.'"

"But I'm not! I'm rapidly running out of money."

"That doesn't matter. Write it down all the same, because you're going to be wealthy. We attract what we think about."

Kevin nodded. "Yes, I know, I know, I know."

"Maybe, but I'll keep reminding you of it until you actually believe it!" Todd looked thoughtfully at Kevin. "Now here's a hard one. Do you seriously want to get back with your wife?"

"Yes, very much."

"Good. Write down 'happily married.'"

"But I'm not!" Kevin grinned at the look on Todd's face. "All right. I'll write it down."

It took twenty minutes for Kevin to write down sixteen things about himself.

"That's enough!" he said, after sucking the pen for a while. "I can't think of anything else."

"That's fine," Todd agreed. He suddenly had a coughing attack and Kevin had to hold him up and pat his back. Kevin was horrified at how frail Todd seemed to be. Once the attack subsided, he passed Todd the glass of water that sat on the cabinet beside the bed. Todd drank deeply. He smiled as he passed the glass back to Kevin.

"That's done me the world of good!" he exclaimed. "Where were we? Yes, I've got it. Now I want you to tell me the first item on your list. Say 'I am whatever it is.' And say it with enthusiasm."

"Okay," Kevin said doubtfully. "I am a human being."

"With enthusiasm!"

"I am a human being!"

"That's better! How did it feel like inside when you said it?"

"Fine." Kevin looked puzzled, but Todd nodded happily.

"Now the next one," he said.

"I am a man!"

"Did that feel all right inside?"

Kevin nodded. "I am Kevin!"

"Feel all right?"

"It felt great!"

"Continue."

Kevin discovered why Todd was asking him how he felt when he came to the sixth item.

"I am wealthy!"

"How did it feel?"

"I'm not sure," Kevin said. His puzzlement was clear in his face as well as his voice.

"Say it again."

"I am wealthy."

"And again, and again, and again."

Kevin had to say the words ten times before he felt comfortable inside.

"That's weird!" he said.

"Your mind sometimes needs time to accept things," Todd told him. "Obviously, you have a sense of poverty consciousness at present. You need to keep on repeating 'I am wealthy' until you can say it without your inner being rejecting it. What's the next one?"

"I am happily married."

"With enthusiasm!"

"I am happily married!"

"That's better. How did it feel?"

"Good! Really good."

Todd smiled. "We're making progress," he said.

It took another twenty minutes to get through the list.

"Now I want you to say that list at least once a day until every single one of those statements sounds right to you."

Kevin saluted. "Yes, sir!"

Todd suddenly doubled up with another coughing fit. Kevin called for Elspeth and together they forced Todd to lie down and rest.

Elspeth pulled the curtains. "That's more than enough for today," she told Todd. "I want you to get some sleep."

"I'm sorry," Kevin said to her in the kitchen. "I shouldn't have stayed."

Elspeth smiled warmly at him.

"No, no. He's been waiting for you all day. He so wants you to get back on your feet again."

"He saved my life."

"I know. He did the same to me."

Kevin stared at her. "You mean...."

"Yes."

"That's incredible!" Kevin walked through to the living room and sat down on the leather couch.

"There are more than us." Elspeth followed him in. She stood by the book shelves, a strange smile on her face. "I think there could be many, judging from all the visitors he gets."

"Kevin!" A faint call summoned Kevin back to Todd's side.

"Sit down, boy." Todd's voice was almost a whisper, but was still commanding. Todd waited until Kevin had made himself comfortable before continuing. "I want to tell you something else."

"Lesson five?"

Todd's eyes gleamed. "You're right. Lesson five!"

Kevin took hold of Todd's hand and gently squeezed it. "I'm ready."

"This one's a hard one. Many people give up on this one. Countless people give up on this. They get so close to reaching their goals and then they give up. It's such a waste."

Kevin nodded and studied the old man's face. It seemed strange to see such young, vibrant eyes in an old, tired, pale face.

"Persistence is number five," Todd said.

Kevin nodded his head. "I'm not surprised."

"If you persist, you can do anything, anything at all. Set your goals high, Kevin, and go after them with relentless determination and persistence. You do that, and there's no way in the world you could possibly fail." A faint smile crossed Todd's face. "I'll rephrase that. You might fail once, twice, or a hundred times, but in the end you'll reap the rewards of success."

The intensity Todd put into his words seemed to tire him. He closed his eyes for several seconds and took a deep breath, but his grasp on Kevin's wrist never faltered.

Just as Kevin decided the old man had fallen asleep, he opened his eyes. They were twinkling and appeared to illuminate his entire face.

"Remember Churchill?"

"Who?"

"Winston Churchill?"

Kevin nodded and smiled. "Sorry, you lost me for a second. Of course I do. And I think I know what you're going to say."

Todd's smile broadened. "Go on then. Say it for me."

Kevin licked his lips as he thought. "Winston Churchill was the ultimate in persistence. During the darkest days of the World War II he told everyone that England would never surrender. He taught an entire country the value of persistence."

Todd nodded. "In spite of deprivations and enormous casualties, the Brits resolved never, ever to surrender. And they won the war."

He let go of Kevin's wrist and patted it a couple of times. "I need to sleep now. Can you come and see me tomorrow after you've had lunch with Sandy?"

———

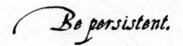

Be persistent.

Chapter
6

"Why did you bring her?" Kevin whispered.

Sandy squeezed his arm. "It's all right. Mum wants to say something to you, then she's leaving."

"She's not having lunch with us?"

"No." Sandy shook her head and grinned. She squeezed his arm again. "Don't look so worried."

All the same, Monica asked the hostess for a table for three, and they were led to the only spare table in the crowded restaurant. Kevin sat opposite her with Sandy beside him. Monica casually took his hand in hers as she sat down.

"I didn't know you were joining us for lunch," Kevin said.

Monica's permanent expression of disapproval creased into a faint smile. "I'm not staying, Kevin. I have shopping to do." She toyed with the menu for a few moments. "Oh, maybe I'll have a coffee while you eat. Duncan and I have been talking about your situation."

Kevin could imagine the two of them endlessly dissecting his "situation."

"You don't need to worry about me," he said. "I've got a number of job interviews. Everything's under control."

Monica's gloved hand reached across the table and tapped him on the wrist. "I'm pleased to hear it. Duncan and I owe you an apology."

Kevin's eyes widened, but he had to wait for enlightenment as the waitress arrived to take their order.

Monica looked at him over her coffee cup. "Yes, as I was saying, Duncan and I feel we might have been a bit harsh the other night."

"Forget it."

"No, Kevin. We want to apologize. We've gone around and around in circles discussing your situation, and we've finally come to an agreement."

"That's good." Kevin looked at Sandy who was examining the border of the tablecloth. "What have you agreed on?"

"We feel that it is your life, Kevin, and you have to do whatever it is you want with it. Of course, as you are married you have responsibilities. You can't just do whatever you wish when you wish. But, if you want to go back into business, after this terrible disaster…" Monica shuddered and took another sip of coffee. "Well, that's your business."

"Thanks, Monica. That's certainly cleared the air."

"And we won't be interfering. Of course, we are only concerned about Sandy."

"Of course."

Monica stood up and came around the table to kiss Sandy goodbye. A note changed hands.

"Lunch is on me," Monica said. "Enjoy yourselves."

They watched her make her way out of the restaurant.

"Did you know she was going to do that?" Kevin asked.

Sandy nodded. "Sort of. They've been talking about it endlessly. I'm not sure that it's what they really want, but they want us to be happy."

Kevin smiled. "An apology. That's amazing, especially from your mother."

"Well, eat up. She's paying for it."

Afterwards, Kevin walked Sandy back to her work. He kissed her outside the entrance to her office block. Sandy giggled.

"This is what it was like before we got married." Her expression changed. "Kevin, I'm thrilled you're looking for a job, but please be careful about seeing this old man with all his funny ideas. Please?"

She kissed him again, and before he could reply, went through the revolving door.

Kevin was delighted to find Todd dressed and outside on his balcony enjoying the sun.

"How did it go?" Todd asked him.

"I'll tell you," Kevin said. "Once you've told me how you are."

Todd smiled. "Pretty good for an old fellow. In a day or two I'll be down there again hugging trees!"

"That's wonderful." Kevin smiled fondly at his friend, and told him about his lunch and Sandy's last words to him.

"She's quite right," Todd said when Kevin had finished. "You do need to be careful."

Kevin licked his lips. "Careful of what?"

"Everything I say. Don't simply accept it. That won't work. You have to go out into the world and test my advice. That way you'll find out if it is good or bad."

"But I know it's good!"

Todd shook his head. "I appreciate your confidence in me, Kevin, but you have to actually do it."

Kevin nodded. "Okay. I'll try."

"No, no, no!" Todd's eyes stared hard at Kevin. "Don't try anything. If you say you're going to try, you'll fail every time. The very word 'try' sets up the expectation of failing."

"I remember you telling me that the word 'try' was not in your vocabulary."

"Now you know why." Todd smiled. "But don't just accept what I say. Put it to the test."

"Is that another stepping stone?"

"No. You're not ready for the next one yet. I'll tell you when the time is right."

———

Chapter 7

At exactly 10:30, Kevin was escorted into Mr. Grayland's office. It was a corner office on the eleventh floor of a downtown tower, and as Kevin walked in, he idly wondered what the annual rent must be.

Mr. Grayland shook him warmly by the hand and asked him to sit down on a small couch at one end of the large room.

"You have an impressive resumé," he said, tapping the papers he held in his hand.

"Thank you," Kevin said. "But I must tell you up front that I am not sure I really want the job."

Mr. Grayland laughed. "I've never heard that before—at least not while interviewing someone."

"Well, Mr. Grayland, I do need a job. I need a job badly. My business collapsed and I owe a great deal of money, so I need a job. But I also need to be fair to you. I intend to become self-employed again just as soon as I can. I'm looking for something to tide me over. I realize that you're probably looking for someone who will stay with your company for years and years."

Mr. Grayland stood up and walked over to the window. He rubbed his chin thoughtfully. After a while he began to chuckle and shake his head. He turned back to Kevin, still chuckling.

"Come here," he said. "I want to show you something."

Kevin joined him at the window and looked down at the intersection below and across at the other tall buildings. It looked like the downtown of any good-sized city.

Mr. Grayland indicated it all with a wave of his hand. "Tell me," he said. "What do you see?"

Kevin looked again. A car horn blared on the street below. He watched the traffic come to a halt to let pedestrians cross the busy street. He was aware that Mr. Grayland was watching him closely.

"I can see many things, Mr. Grayland," he said. "But I see one thing above all. That is opportunity.

Everyone down there in the street, everyone in each of those cars, and everyone in each of the offices all around us needs something. It's a world of opportunity."

Mr. Grayland beamed at him. "You know, young man," he said. "I think we can help each other."

Two hours later, Kevin sat across the dining room table from Todd and told him about his morning. The robe Todd was wearing over his pajamas seemed several sizes too large, but his face was as alert and interested as ever.

"We seemed to hit it off from the very start," Kevin said. "I told him what you told me about opportunity being everywhere, and he ended up giving me an opportunity. I'm starting up a new division for his company, providing all the peripherals for computers. It ties in my computer knowledge with their stationery and office product expertise."

Todd beamed and spread his hands in excitement. "That's wonderful! See what happens when you hug life and keep alert for opportunities. When do you start?"

"Any time I want. I've decided to start on Monday. That will give me a chance to tidy up a few things first. The great thing is that it's almost like having my own business. We'll be partners, but I'll also have some regular money coming in while we get it established."

Todd took a mouthful of mushroom soup. Kevin watched Todd's hand shake slightly as he carefully maneuvered the spoon to his mouth. At least he was eating. Up until now he'd simply played with his soup.

"I want to thank you so much," Kevin said. "For everything."

Todd shook his head. "There's no need. I'm as happy for you as you are. I've planted a few seeds and now they're bearing fruit. The pleasure is all mine."

Kevin helped himself to some ham and salad. "I wish I could repay you in some way."

Todd grinned. "You can, and I'm sure you will. All you need do is help someone else, the way you say I helped you. You've already begun. Remember that tramp in the park? I couldn't have been happier when you told me what you did for him."

"He didn't appreciate it."

"So what? You did a good thing. You created good karma for yourself. Who knows, maybe that's why you got this wonderful offer this morning."

Kevin put down his fork. "You think that I got this offer because I helped the man in the park?"

Todd waved his hands. "Maybe, maybe not. But the mere fact that you did good means that good will someday, somehow, come back to you. It's a universal law. You don't have to believe it for it to work. I know myself that it is almost a selfish thing. I help others because I know that I'll benefit myself in so many different ways."

"How have you benefited by helping me?"

Todd laughed. "I've had enormous enjoyment from your company and friendship. You've stimulated my mind. I'm as happy as you are about your new opportunity. I've been richly rewarded already."

"Yes, but in other ways?"

Todd sighed and placed his spoon down inside the soup bowl. "I'm sure there will be many ways, but they are not always recognizable at the time. You know, when something nice happens when you least expect it. I have those all the time, and I have no doubt that I experience them purely because of things I have done to help others in the past."

There was a long silence while Kevin thought about Todd's words. Elspeth bustled in and replenished the fruit juice and took away the empty plates. Kevin noticed her hand lingered on Todd's shoulder.

Todd ate some salad and drank his juice.

"Now it's time to tell you rule number six." Todd smiled impishly at Kevin, his face suddenly young and youthful. "In fact, you already know and practice this one."

"Thank goodness for that!" Kevin laughed. "I can't believe I've been practicing one all along and didn't even know it!"

"I wouldn't exactly say that," Todd corrected. "This is something you used to know, but then forgot. However, I think today you found it again."

With effort, Todd pulled himself away from the table and stood up on shaky feet. Kevin went around to help support him. Together they walked out to the balcony overlooking the harbor. Todd sat down in a padded deck chair and Kevin brought a dining table chair out to sit on. Kevin took several deep breaths of the sea air before sitting down.

"Don't keep me in suspense," he said. "What is rule number six?"

"Do you believe in God?" Todd asked, his eyes fixed on Kevin's face.

Kevin gulped. "I'm, I'm not really sure, Todd. I believe in something—call it a universal life force, or spirit that's inside each of us."

Todd nodded. "That's close enough, I guess. Yes, I believe in a universal mind and a little spark that lives inside every living thing. We're all inter-connected, you know. Every living thing on this planet. That's why we need to look after everything in this beautiful world. At its most basic, it is all part of us."

Todd watched the white tops riding the gentle waves of the harbor. "Faith is what we all need, Kevin," he said. "I don't mean it in a sense of believing in a god sitting on a fluffy cloud some-where. What I mean is, you must believe in your-self. You must have faith—confidence if you like—that you can accomplish the goals you seek. If you believe in yourself you can do anything."

Kevin sighed heavily. "Do you really think I believe in myself?"

"Of course you do. Yesterday you didn't, but this morning you sold yourself to Mr. Grayland. You couldn't have done that if you hadn't believed in yourself. Remember when you first began in business? You must have been full of confidence and belief then."

"Look what good it did me."

Todd laughed. "Yes, you lost your confidence for a short while. It doesn't matter. You have it back again now."

"So I've just one more lesson to learn?"

Todd nodded. "You already know it, Kevin."

"Will you tell it to me now?"

Todd shook his head gravely. "Not today. I want you to practice the other ones a little bit more. I don't want you to simply think about them and accept them on an intellectual level. I want you to practice them in everyday life. That way you'll be able to prove them to your own satisfaction. Maybe even to Sandy's satisfaction, too." Todd reached across and touched Kevin's knee. "I'm feeling a bit cold. Could you ask Elspeth to bring me a blanket?"

————————

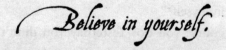

Believe in yourself.

Chapter
8

The insistent ring of his front doorbell woke Kevin. He reached for the bedside clock and discovered it was ten past nine. He scrambled out of bed, hastily put on his robe and ran to the door. Two policeman stood stiffly at attention, allowing no expression to cross their faces as they looked him up and down. They introduced themselves and asked if they could have a few words.

"Er, come inside," Kevin said. He stood aside to allow them in and then led the way to the living room.

"You've come about my complaint," Kevin said. "I'm sorry, I should have withdrawn it."

The older of the two policemen, a swarthy-faced man of about Kevin's age, opened up a notebook.

"You made a complaint about a Mr. Michael Bestens."

"Yes. He used to be my business partner. But I want to withdraw that complaint."

"You said that on April 15th he viciously attacked you with a baseball bat, in front of several witnesses."

"It was just an argument that got out of hand. He didn't hurt me."

"You spent one night in hospital and the medical report reveals you had two broken ribs."

"Yes. Well, I'm better now."

"The witnesses corroborate your story, Mr. Huddersfield. It was obviously a serious, unprovoked attack."

"Well, our business had just collapsed and I blamed him. I thought he had stolen money from the business."

"It's surprising that he was the one attacking you, in that case," the policeman observed.

"I guess I'd provoked him. I accused him of all sorts of things, in front of mutual friends."

"Those mutual friends corroborated your account of the incident."

"Yes." Kevin tightened the cord on his robe. The bare, wooden floor was cold beneath his feet. "Look, can't I just withdraw the complaint? I've forgiven him. In fact, I'd almost forgotten about that evening till I saw you standing on the doorstep."

The younger policeman clicked his tongue and looked up to the ceiling. His colleague closed his notebook.

"What about the alleged theft of money from the business? Have you made a complaint about that?"

Kevin shook his head. "No. I was going to. In fact I asked my accountant to check it out and determine the exact amount of the discrepancy. But I've decided to let it go. I've forgiven my partner and forgotten about the matter."

The policeman drummed his fingers on the closed notebook. "It's not that easy, Mr. Huddersfield. You made a complaint and we've put time and effort into checking it out. Now, at this late stage, you want us to forget all about it?"

Kevin cleared his throat. "Yes, yes, please. If it's possible."

The policemen stood up in unison. The older one shook his head. "Our job would be so much easier if everyone was as forgiving as you," he said.

"I try and live for today," Kevin explained. "Yesterday is gone."

The two men exchanged glances and made a hasty exit.

Kevin dressed quickly and made himself some strong coffee. After a few gulps of the scalding liquid, he reached for the phone and called his ex-partner.

"Hi, Michael," he said. He could imagine the startled look on his ex-partner's face. The silence lasted several seconds and was broken by Kevin. "It's Kevin here, Michael. Just calling to see how you are."

"Fine, just great," Michael replied, surprise very evident in his voice. "How're you doing?"

"Good," Kevin said. "Every morning life starts anew. I just called to say hello and to tell you I've withdrawn those charges. I also forgive you. I forgive you for everything."

"What?"

"Have a great life, Michael. Bye."

Kevin smiled at himself in the mirror as he shaved. Todd's philosophy of life certainly works, he thought. I feel better than I've felt in years.

He felt a sudden urge to tell Todd about his morning. Todd's phone line was busy and, after trying several times, Kevin decided to walk over to see how he was.

It was a cloudy, overcast day but Kevin's spirits were high. He smiled at a mother and toddler he passed on the street, and hugged two trees in a park. Once he laughed out loud at the sheer exhilaration of being alive.

There was no answer when he rang Todd's doorbell. Kevin stood indecisively by the door for some minutes and then walked slowly toward the waterfront stores.

He ordered a cappuccino at an outdoor cafe and sat where he could see the entrance to Todd's building. He felt a slight twinge of concern as he nursed the warm cup between his hands. Thirty minutes later he ordered another coffee and made it last for an hour. No one came in or out of Todd's building.

Kevin felt tension building up in his shoulders and he paced up and down the sidewalk outside the building. He wished he knew Elspeth's address.

Inspiration struck and he pressed the doorbells of the other apartment owners. One answered, a crackly, disembodied voice that sounded ghostlike over the intercom. It seemed to belong to an elderly woman. She knew nothing, she told him, but would knock on Todd's door and see if there was any reply.

It took ages for her to come back. Her husband, she told him, had seen an ambulance pull up during the night, but she didn't know if it had called for Mr. Melvin. There was no response to her knocking on his door.

Kevin thanked her and turned away. He felt as if he were in a dense fog and leaned against a brick wall for support. He'd have to call all the hospitals and find out where Todd was.

"Don't cry," a familiar voice said. He looked around and grinned in relief when he saw Elspeth. She rested her hand on his shoulder. "He'll be home this afternoon. Will you help me take the groceries upstairs?"

Todd had had a seizure during the night, she told him. She had stayed overnight in his apartment as he wasn't well, and it was fortunate she had as she was able to call for an ambulance.

"He's ready to move on," she told Kevin, gazing into his eyes. "There's just you and one other holding him back."

"I don't want to hold him back," Kevin said.

Elspeth smiled. "Of course you don't. But he can't move on until he knows you'll be all right."

Kevin rubbed his eyes. "I'll be okay," he said. "It's just that I've never met anyone like Todd before. I don't want to lose him so soon after finding him."

"None of us want to lose him," Elspeth said. "But he's old and he's tired."

"I know, I'm thinking only of myself."

Elspeth shook her head. "I know just how you feel, Kevin. Believe me—I do."

"Who's the other person?"

"It's a woman who just lost her husband. Todd's been helping her for the last few weeks."

"At the same time he's been helping me?"

Elspeth nodded. Kevin noticed tears in her eyes.

"Will he be all right?" Kevin asked. "You said he's coming home this afternoon."

"He'll need plenty of rest." Elspeth stood up and began putting the groceries away.

Kevin felt helpless. "Is there anything I can do?"

"What are you like at vacuuming?"

The apartment was immaculate when the ambulance pulled up outside. Elspeth had bought flowers and their delicate scent perfumed the living room.

Kevin and Elspeth ran downstairs to see if they could help. Todd was pleased to see them. His face was pale and gaunt, but his smile was warm. "Thank you both so much," he said.

The paramedics carried him upstairs and put him to bed. Elspeth had hot soup ready, which she spoon-fed him. Kevin sat on the end of the bed feeling sadder than he had ever felt in his whole life.

"You're not doing it," Todd told him.

Kevin was startled. "Not doing what?"

"Rule number one."

"Live for today," Kevin repeated automatically. His eyes met Todd's and he smiled. "You're right," he said. "But it's hard."

"Life's not meant to be easy," Todd reminded him. "But you're strong, you're capable and you're going to win."

Kevin nodded. "Thank you."

"Tell me about your day."

Kevin's enthusiasm grew as he told Todd about his morning. Todd smiled and nodded. "You're well on the way," he said. He stared at Kevin for a long time, a faint smile lingering on his lips.

"Get better," Kevin said. "Please. We all need you."

"Thanks. But it's time for me to move on. You know my philosophy now. I've no fear of the future. And you shouldn't have, either. Not now."

Kevin stood up. "I'd better go now. But I'll be back in the morning." Kevin paused at the door and looked back at the frail man in the large bed.

"Kevin."

"Yes."

"There's one more lesson."

"I know."

"You've been practicing it this morning. I'm very proud of you."

Kevin smiled. He tried to think what it could be. "You'll have to tell me," he said.

"You have to help others, and you must forgive others."

Kevin nodded slowly. "I see."

"There's more." Todd pulled himself up until he was almost sitting. He struggled for breath, but waved Kevin away as he rushed to help. "First of all, Kevin, you must forgive yourself."

"Forgive myself?" Kevin frowned as he tried to understand.

"We all do lots of silly, stupid things," Todd said between wheezes. "We're all thoughtless, unkind, mean, intolerant—all sorts of things. You need to forgive yourself for all the things you've done in the past. Only when you've done that can you really help others."

Kevin licked his lips. "So I've forgiven my partner. Can I not really forgive him until I've forgiven myself?"

"Yes and no." Kevin could see how much effort this was costing the old man, but he knew he could not leave until Todd had explained it all to him.

"When you forgave him," Todd said, "did you feel a huge weight fall off your shoulders?"

Kevin laughed. "I certainly did!"

Todd nodded. "Try forgiving yourself. You'll feel completely reborn. When you forgive yourself you are really practicing lesson one, aren't you?"

"You mean 'yesterday is gone'?"

"That's it. Think about it, Kevin." Todd yawned and smiled sleepily at Kevin. "I'm sorry. The trip home must have exhausted me. Will you come and see me again tomorrow?"

As if on cue, Elspeth appeared and ushered Kevin away. At the door, Kevin wrote down his phone number.

"Call me, Elspeth. Please call me if anything happens, or if I can help. I'm going straight home now. Call anytime at all."

Kevin found it hard to sit still at home. He kept wondering how Todd was. After he had phoned Elspeth for the third time, she told him that she would leave the receiver off if he did not stop calling.

"I'll call you if anything happens," she said. "I promise."

In the afternoon, Kevin walked to a shopping mall and bought some parchment paper, ink, and a calligraphy pen. He sat down at the kitchen table and practiced writing letters on a scrap piece of paper, trying to make them look exactly like the three words in the book in Todd's spare bedroom. After half an hour he felt reasonably confident and began writing on a sheet of parchment. He headed it: "The Seven Secrets to Success."

He looked at his handiwork critically. It wasn't perfect, but it was reasonably close to the style he remembered.

Carefully, he wrote down "Yesterday is gone." He could recall every emotion, feeling, and nuance that he had felt upon first opening the book and reading those words. Kevin smiled. They were the words that had started to change his life. Tentatively, he said the words out loud. Yes, they felt right. No matter what other people might think or say, these words were the absolute truth for Kevin.

It took several minutes to decide on the final wording for the second stepping stone. "Hug life" was probably what Todd had meant, but Kevin eventually wrote down "Hug trees, and life." He found himself nodding agreement with these words as he finished writing them. Again, he said the words out loud to see if they rang true for him. He stood up and walked around the room saying the words over and over. He laughed at his reflection in the mirror and returned to work.

"Set worthwhile goals" was easier to write down than to put into practice, but Kevin felt pleased that, with Todd's help, he had set some specific goals for himself.

When he wrote down "Opportunities are everywhere," he felt as if he was back on the busy street with Todd looking at the stores and the passing cars. He wondered if he and Todd would ever walk together along that street again. Before he got too maudlin, his mind provided him with an image of his interview with Mr. Grayland, where he had used much the same words to sell himself.

"Be persistent" was the fifth stepping stone. He had to say it aloud twenty times before it began to feel right.

"I need persistence, persistence, persistence," he told himself. "Persistence ensures success."

Kevin paused to make himself a cup of tea before continuing. He needed time to think about the sixth stepping stone. Would the word "faith" be sufficient, or should he write "faith in oneself"?

As he enjoyed his afternoon tea he read and reread the stepping stones he had already written down. When he had finished, he picked up the pen and wrote "Faith."

"Faith," he said out loud. "Faith," he repeated more tentatively. He shook his head and added two more words.

"Faith in myself," he read out loud. "Faith in myself." That sounded better.

There was just one stepping stone left. Kevin looked critically at what he had written so far. He had room on the page to allow two lines for the last one, and still keep the proportions the way he wanted them.

He found it harder to write down the last one. He was grateful, but at the same time saddened to think that Todd had given him the complete list. He had been so keen to learn them all, but now that he had, he would have loved to have several more still ahead.

So far, his calligraphy had been reasonably good. He was surprised at how this old skill had come back. With the last one, he took extra care as he did not want to ruin his work with a careless stroke of the pen.

Slowly he wrote: "Help others. Forgive others and forgive myself."

It was almost dark when he finished. He heated up some spaghetti and ate it while watching television. Several times he wanted to call Elspeth, but held himself back.

He went to bed early, and lay in the dark, silently repeating Todd's rules to himself, over and over again, like a mantra.

Before drifting off to sleep he tried to forgive himself, the way Todd had told him. It was hard and he was about to give up when he felt a release that was almost spiritual. He felt weightless and at perfect peace with the world. This is what Todd meant, he told himself as he rolled over and fell asleep.

The phone woke him on the second ring. He grabbed the receiver with a sudden feeling of terror.

"Is that you, Elspeth?" he asked.

"Come quickly," Elspeth said. "His time is here."

"I'm on my way."

He called for a cab and had just enough time to get shaved and dressed before it arrived. They arrived at Todd's home at the same time as an ambulance.

Kevin followed the paramedics upstairs. Elspeth stood at the open door, tears running down her face. Kevin stopped, two steps from the top. There was no point in going any further.

Help others — forgive them, and yourself.

Chapter 9

Mr. Grayland smiled at the expression on Kevin's face.

"This is just the start," he said. "I figure that you'll need at least this much room. We have more space if you need it, but this should be enough to begin with."

"It's perfect." Kevin gazed around the empty warehouse. "I guess we'll fill this in no time."

"The shelving arrives this afternoon," Mr. Grayland said. "In the meantime you can go through these catalogs and see what you need. I've assigned a young guy to help you. His name's Josh. He's a good worker, and I'm sure he'll do a good job for you. I also have a feeling he'll benefit from being with you."

Kevin thought about Mr. Grayland's words as he was introduced to Josh an hour later. He was a tall, well-built teenager with ginger-colored hair that reached to his shoulders. He gave a shy smile and made little eye contact as he met Kevin.

They went through the catalogs together. Kevin was impressed at the young man's knowledge.

After lunch, Kevin asked him to draw up a floor plan indicating where the shelving was to go.

"That's good," Kevin told him when it was done. "When the delivery men arrive would you get them to place the shelving according to that plan?"

Josh lowered his head. "I couldn't," he mumbled.

"Of course you can," Kevin said. "I have to go out, so you'll be in charge."

Josh licked his lips. "I, I don't think I could do it."

Kevin nodded. "Sit down for a moment," he said. Briefly, he told Josh of his business failure and his life-changing meeting with Todd. "Todd taught me about faith," he said. "You must have faith in yourself. If you believe you can do it, you can. You did a wonderful job doing the layout. All you need do now is make sure that the shelving is put in the right position. I know you can do that. Mr. Grayland is confident you can do it. What do you feel?"

Josh shifted uncomfortably. "I can do it."

When Kevin and Mr. Grayland returned from visiting their main supplier a few hours later, all the shelving was up. Josh greeted them with a wide grin.

"You timed that well," he said. "The men just left."

He was keen to take Kevin on a tour of inspection.

"We could store everything to do with printers in this row here," he said. "All the laser cartridges and other odds and ends can go over here, so they're close together. In the next bay we could store our modems."

Kevin smiled at Josh's enthusiasm as he completed the tour.

"We'll do it," he said. "Put it all down on your plan, so Mr. Grayland and I will know where everything is to go. Our first stock arrives tomorrow. I won't be here." Kevin's voice trailed off as he realized that it was Todd's funeral in the morning. "I'll be in later on in the day, but you'll be in charge until I get here."

"In charge?"

"Yes, Josh. Faith in yourself, remember?"

"But Kevin, the last time Mr. Grayland put me in charge everything went wrong."

"Yesterday is gone." The words came out automatically, and Kevin blinked as he realized what he had said. Todd's words were becoming part of his life! Josh was looking at him blankly.

"What I mean by that, Josh, is that the time everything went wrong was in the past. You must let go of the past, and live for today. We've all made mistakes. We all have regrets. We have to let go of all that old baggage that we no longer need. You'll feel so much better about yourself once you do."

Josh nodded slowly. "You're trying to talk me into being in charge tomorrow?"

"Yes, Josh. But only because I know you can do it. I have faith in you."

Josh shook his head. "I hope I can do it," he said doubtfully.

"Let go of the past, Josh!"

As he went to bed that night, Kevin was still wondering how Todd's words came so easily to his lips. Maybe he was starting to live his life according to Todd's stepping stones. If he could help Josh gain some confidence and self-esteem, he'd be helping someone else, in the same way Todd had helped him.

Kevin fell asleep with a smile on his face.

———————

Chapter 10

Kevin was amazed at the number of people who turned out for Todd's funeral. It was a bleak, wintry day with sudden squalls of rain. Despite this, the cathedral was filled to overflowing with mourners, wanting to pay their last respects to their friend. Many people stood outside in the cold and wet while the funeral service was conducted.

Kevin sat in the middle of the church. Sandy sat beside him and held his hand throughout the service. Kevin paid little attention to what was going on. Like many of the other mourners he used the time to think about the miraculous transformation that Todd had made in his life.

Several people stood up and paid tribute to their friend. Kevin was astonished to find their stories were very close to his. Todd had obviously helped almost everyone in the church at some stage in their lives.

Even the minister seemed to have been touched by Todd. He gave a glowing eulogy telling the congregation about his experiences with Todd and how Todd had transformed his life.

"Everyone who met him," he concluded, "went away a better person for having known our dear friend."

There was a pause in the rain when the service ended and the mourners slowly went outside and mingled in the attractive surroundings.

Outside, Kevin found a few of his old work colleagues. They were eager to discuss their relationship with Todd. He was surprised to find that people who he had considered to be happy and well adjusted had at different times met Todd when they most needed to find him.

Sandy had been moved by the service, particularly the tributes, and she listened closely as the people that Kevin spoke with told of their experiences with Todd.

that is why I've asked you all back here." She looked around the room, a gentle smile on her face. "When Todd knew he was dying, some months ago, he decided to found a trust to keep his work alive. He has left his considerable fortune to this trust, and we, the founding committee, believe we can do an excellent job of helping people, using just the interest from Todd's investments. But we need people. Helping people was Todd's passion. He was there for every one of us when we needed it most, and now he needs our help. Are any of you prepared to help get this project off the ground?"

Kevin found himself nodding enthusiastically. He looked around the room and saw everyone had a hand held up high. Kevin immediately raised his hand, too.

"Thank you," Elspeth said. "I knew we'd chosen wisely."

"Todd and I formed a small committee, all of whom are here. Together, we selected the rest of you because of your particular talents and skills."

She seemed to be looking directly at Kevin. He frowned as he tried to think what skills he possessed to work on a project of this size.

"I am the temporary chairperson. However, once you have received our requests and decided that you wish to help, we will have an election of officers. Of course, if you do not wish to be part of this, for any reason whatsoever, you are free to leave at any time. I promise that none of us will lose respect for you if you do choose to leave. Mr. Ambrose has an envelope for each of you. Please read the letter inside and let us know if you can help. You each have a specific task to do. Get your letter now and we'll continue in five minutes."

Mr. Ambrose turned out to be the elderly man who was serving drinks. Kevin waited in line to receive his letter and thought about Elspeth. To think that he'd considered her to be simply Todd's housekeeper. Todd had obviously been grooming her for this role.

Kevin took his envelope through to the bedroom where he had slept the night he met Todd. He opened the drawer in the bedside cabinet and removed the book inside. He passed his hand over the embossed cover before opening it to read the words he knew so well: "Yesterday is gone."

And Todd has gone too, he thought. Instead of sadness, a sense of peace descended on him, a feeling so beautiful and perfect in its tranquility that it brought tears to his eyes. He knew then that Todd had not gone, that he could draw on Todd's essence whenever he wished.

He sat down on the bed and opened the envelope. To his surprise the letter was in Todd's handwriting. Had Todd written personal letters to all the others?

"My dear Kevin," he read. "By the time you read this I'll be dead and buried, but you know my beliefs and philosophy. I've never believed that death is the end, so do not grieve for me. I'm just starting on the most exciting adventure of all. I'll miss our talks, though. They meant as much to me as they did to you. You kept thanking me, when I should have been thanking you. I knew my time here was coming to a close when you came into my life. The extra weeks that you gave me allowed me time to work on this foundation and I hope you'll agree to be part of it.

"You mentioned that you started your working life as a journalist. Would you be willing to write a small book about your experiences to help others? I'm sure it would help many, many people—much more than we could ever reach on a one-to-one basis. I don't want you to do it right away. I'd like you to consider it first. Then, once you are leading a happy, fulfilling life again, you may want to do it. Please consider this idea seriously.

"You may think I'm gone, Kevin, but I'm not. Whenever you see sunlight glistening on a drop of dew, or see a rainbow, or feel moved by a piece of music, you'll know that I'm there. Bless you, Kevin, and thanks for being my friend. Todd."

Kevin slowly folded the sheet of paper and held it to his heart.

A movement at the door caught his eye and Elspeth came in. He could see that she had been crying.

"We're ready to start again," she told him.

Kevin nodded and returned to the living room. Everybody was more subdued than before and a few were crying openly. Todd must have written a personal letter to everyone here, Kevin thought.

Elspeth tried to smile but found it too hard to manage. She sniffled and blew her nose.

"I guess we've all had a moving few minutes," she said. "I knew what was in every envelope except my own, and I must admit Todd caught me by surprise. I'm sure he did the same to all of you."

She dabbed at a tear with a tissue. Mr. Ambrose came up and put his arms around her. He whispered something to her and she nodded.

Mr. Ambrose kept his arm around her waist. "Ladies and gentlemen," he said. "We've all been given a challenge. I think we should feel honored that Todd chose us to be his successors. Now, not all of you may want to be part of this. If so, that's fine. You can leave now and we thank you for attending."

No one moved. Mr. Ambrose's eyes slowly traversed the room, making eye contact with everyone. Finally he nodded.

"That's good. Todd chose well. I really don't feel we can do much today as we're all feeling overwrought and emotional. Todd asked Elspeth and me to organize the first meeting. We'll contact you all and arrange a suitable time. At that time we'll elect the officers and start work. It's going to be hard work, I can promise you that. It'll be challenging and will stretch us all. But it's also going to be extremely rewarding. Todd helped every one of us when we were at our lowest. Now it's our turn to help others. Goodbye, my friends. I'll see you all in the next week or two."

It took an hour for everyone to leave. Kevin went around the room, introducing himself to the others and exchanging accounts of how Todd had helped everyone there.

Finally, just Elspeth and Kevin remained.

As they cleaned the dishes, Kevin asked Elspeth why Todd had chosen him.

"There must have been a thousand people at the funeral," he said. "Todd could have picked any of them."

Elspeth smiled. "He chose you for many reasons," she said. "First, because you are capable of writing the book."

"And...."

"Mainly because he felt that by helping others you'd become alive again. And you are, Kevin. I saw it just now when you mixed and mingled with everyone. I never knew the old Kevin, but I'd be willing to bet that you're almost back to your old self again."

Kevin shook his head. "No, I'll never be the old Kevin again. He was selfish, egotistical and greedy. Todd helped me change all that. It's not complete yet, but I know I'm on the right track." Kevin put the last plate in the dishwasher and turned it on. "Elspeth," he said. "Something's strange. Even though this is the day of Todd's funeral I feel more alive than I've ever been. In some way I've been transformed."

"We all have," Elspeth agreed. She wiped the counter down and looked critically around the kitchen. "I think we're all done here, Kevin. What are you going to do now?"

"I'm going to have dinner with Sandy. I'm going to ask her to come back home. I've been putting it off for so long, for too long."

"She must be amazed at the change in you."

"Well, if she'll have me back, I'm going to make it work this time. It was all my fault that it ended."

"But that was yesterday."

Kevin laughed. "If I'm going to write the book I'd better practice what it preaches."

"Let me know how you get on."

"Will do. I'll call you tomorrow." Kevin kissed Elspeth on the cheek. "Thank you, thank you, thank you."

Elspeth stopped him at the door.

"Kevin, take this." She lifted up the ceramic rabbit on the mantelpiece and picked up the envelope containing Kevin's goals. Kevin took it from her with a smile.

"You know," he said. "It sounds amazing to me, but I'm already working on all the things I wrote down."

The rain had turned into a mist, and the air smelled fresh and clean. Kevin walked along the street, feeling lightheaded. He tried to analyze his feelings, but it was impossible. He felt devastated at losing Todd, but was also happy as Todd had obviously been ready to move on. Kevin felt certain that wherever Todd was, he'd be helping people who needed him. In his heart, Kevin realized that Todd would always be with him. He felt grateful that he had been given the opportunity to work with the others to establish the foundation and keep Todd's philosophy alive.

He hugged a tree on a busy intersection and waved cheerfully to the startled motorists. Life was good. Life was for living, and with Todd's seven stepping stones to guide him, life would continue to get better and better.

———

Yesterday is gone.

Hug trees, and life.

Set worthwhile goals.

Opportunities are everywhere.

Be persistent.

Believe in yourself.

Help others – forgive them, and yourself.

STAY IN TOUCH

Llewellyn publishes hundreds of books on your favorite subjects. On the following pages you will find listed some books now available on related subjects. Your local bookstore stocks most of these and will stock new Llewellyn titles as they become available. We urge your patronage.

Order by Phone

Call toll-free within the U.S. and Canada, 1–800–THE MOON.
In Minnesota call (612) 291–1970.
We accept Visa, MasterCard, and American Express.

Order by Mail

Send the full price of your order (MN residents add 7% sales tax) in U.S. funds to:

> Llewellyn Worldwide
> P.O. Box 64383, Dept. K797–8
> St. Paul, MN 55164–0383, U.S.A.

Postage and Handling

- $4.00 for orders $15.00 and under
- $5.00 for orders over $15.00
- No charge for orders over $100.00

We ship UPS in the continental United States. We cannot ship to P.O. boxes. Orders shipped to Alaska, Hawaii, Canada, Mexico, and Puerto Rico will be sent first-class mail.
International orders: Airmail—add freight equal to price of each book to the total price of order, plus $5.00 for each non-book item (audiotapes, etc.). **Surface mail**—add $1.00 per item. Allow 4–6 weeks delivery on all orders. Postage and handling rates subject to change.

Group Discounts

We offer a 20% quantity discount to group leaders or agents. You must order a minimum of 5 copies of the same book to get our special quantity price.

Free Catalog

Get a free copy of our color catalog, *New Worlds of Mind and Spirit*. Subscribe for just $10.00 in the United States and Canada ($20.00 overseas, first-class mail). Many bookstores carry *New Worlds*—ask for it.

**FENG SHUI FOR
BEGINNERS**
**Successful Living
by Design**

Richard Webster

Not advancing fast enough
in your career? Maybe your
desk is located in a "negative
position." Wish you had a
more peaceful family life?
Hang a mirror in your dining room and watch what
happens. Is money flowing out of your life rather than
into it? You may want to look to the construction of
your staircase!

For thousands of years, the ancient art of feng shui
has helped people harness universal forces and lead lives
rich in good health, wealth and happiness. The basic
techniques in *Feng Shui for Beginners* are very simple,
and you can put them into place immediately in your
home and work environments. Gain peace of mind, a
quiet confidence, and turn adversity to your advantage
with feng shui remedies.

**1-56718-803-6, 240 pp., 5¼ x 8, photos,
diagrams, softcover**   **$12.95**

DOWSING FOR BEGINNERS
The Art of Discovering: Water, Treasure, Gold, Oil, Artifacts

Richard Webster

This book provides everything you need to know to become a successful dowser. Dowsing is the process of using a dowsing rod or pendulum to divine for anything you wish to locate: water, oil, gold, ancient ruins, lost objects or even missing people. Dowsing can also be used to determine if something is safe to eat or drink, or to diagnose and treat allergies and diseases.

Learn about the tools you'll use: angle and divining rods, pendulums, wands—even your own hands and body can be used as dowsing tools! Explore basic and advanced dowsing techniques, beginning with methods for dowsing the terrain for water. Find how to dowse anywhere in the world without leaving your living room, with the technique of map dowsing. Discover the secrets of dowsing to determine optimum planting locations; to monitor your pets' health and well-being; to detect harmful radiation in your environment; to diagnose disease; to determine psychic potential; to locate archeological remains; to gain insight into yourself, and more! *Dowsing for Beginners* is a complete "how-to-do-it" guide to learning an invaluable skill.

1-56718-802-8, 256 pp., 5¼ x 8, illus., photos, softcover $12.95

REVEALING HANDS
How to Read Palms

Richard Webster

Palmistry has been an accurate tool for self-knowledge and prediction for thousands of years. The ability to read palms can lead you to a better understanding of yourself, as well as the complex motivations of other people. Guide and advise others in a sensitive and caring manner, determine compatibility between couples, and help people decide what type of career suits them best.

Revealing Hands makes it easier than ever to learn the science of palmistry. As soon as you complete the first chapter, you can begin reading palms with confidence and expertise. Professional palmist and teacher Richard Webster leads you step by step through the subject with clear explanations and life-size hand drawings that highlight the points being covered. He provides sample scripts that can serve as a foundation for your readings for others, and he answers all of the questions he has been asked by his students over the years. Whether you are interested in taking up palmistry professionally or just for fun, you will find the information in this book exceptionally entertaining and easy to use.

0-87542-870-3, 304 pp., 7 x 10, 117 illus., softcover   **$14.95**